Nostalgia

BLISSFUL MOMENTS

Rajani Suryanarayana

BookLeaf
Publishing

India | USA | UK

Made with ❤ on the BookLeaf Publishing Platform
www.bookleafpub.in
www.bookleafpub.com

Dedication

This book is wholeheartedly dedicated to my cherished husband and children, whose unwavering love and support have illuminated my path. To all those who have journeyed alongside me in life, your love and kindness are intricately woven into every page of *Nostalgia*.

This collection is a heartfelt tribute to the joy of poetry and the exquisite beauty found in life's simplest moments. May it resonate with each of you.

Preface

This book is my first book book of poems. Each poem is
very close to my heart. each word is from my heart.
These are precious qualities and moments we all have
around us, which we seldom notice. This book is a
thank-you note for all these wonderful moments. I am
Grateful to My Krishna, My parents, My Husband and
Children for all the beautiful moments which I
experience in my day to day life. They are my courage,
faith and hope who bring smile on my face, accepting me
with all my imperfections,

Acknowledgements

I would like to express my heartfelt gratitude to My Krishna, for making this this book possible. To my family, whose unwavering love, patience, and encouragement have been my constant pillars of support, thank you for always believing in me, even when I doubted myself. A special thanks to my children whose insightful feedback and guidance have helped shape my writing.

I also wish to extend my deep appreciation to Miss Aastha and the entire team at BookLeaf Publishing for their professionalism, attention to detail, and commitment in bringing my vision to life. Without their support, this book would not have come into being.

I am truly grateful for everyone who has touched my life

2. It's me Jojo

I hear your car's familiar sound,
The locking beep, a joy profound;
I sense the gate swing wide and free,
And know you're climbing steps to me.

With eager heart, I wait at door,
I leap and roll, a joyful race;
My tiny paws, they long to greet,
As my wagging tail dances in beat.

For I am Jojo, your little friend,
In this warm home, our love won't end;
I cherish you more than you can see,
In every bark, it's clear to me.

If I could speak, oh what a delight,
With laughter and love,
I'd share day and night!

1. Krishna

Krishna, what am I without your grace,
In the ocean of life, I wander like a wave
Hold my hand, in every crest and trough
Through every step, as my life unfolds.

Guide me gently, steady in my way,
With every doubt, be my guiding light
In thoughts that weigh, help me softly pray,
For in your light, I just know the way.

The journey full of mountains and valleys,
Yet in your might, I gather all my strength
With you beside me, worries fade to sleep,
Your smile chases darkness into light.

In your lovely presence Krishna
Flowers bloom vibrant and bright,
like stories of our lives unfold.
A dance of colours on the earth embrace

Every blossom, echoes your grace
The marigold whispers in golden hues,
While jasmine entwines with the moon
As if nature thrives in your flute's melodies...

3. Gratitude

As dawn awakes, the birds begin to sing,
Their melodies weave dreams in morning light.
The sky, a canvas where colours fling ,
As sunlight dances, breaking through the night.

The breeze arrives, as gentle thoughtful friend,
It whispers softly, carrying the dew.
Each drop unwinds the burdens we can't mend,
Reviving spirits, fresh as morning's hue.

From farms, the milk still warm, a simple grace,
And coffee brews, it's fragrance fills the space
On plates, warm food brings comfort in its place,
While evening tea finds sunsets grace

As flowers bloom, filling in colours and frangnace
Moon and stars, playing hide and seek forms a maze
With family near, love and warmth surrounds my heart,
Oh, Universe, thank you for every part.

4. Wonders of the night

As the sun folds into the horizon,
the moon climbs, silver and soft,
holding court over the night.
White flowers bloom, tiny lanterns, among dark green
leaves,
like stars sprinkled on the earth,
a gentle glow in the shadows.

The air is rich
touched with their sweet perfume,
pulling away to whisper secrets of another world,
where noise of the day becomes a memory.

Beneath a sky dotted with light
crickets sing their beautiful melodies,
a steady rhythm that lulls the heart,
as breeze pushes the day to the past
cool and comforting,
carrying scent and sound,
lifting us above day's trials.

Here, we shed our masks,
no more roles to play,
just souls in clear night air,
dancing in silence, lost in moments,
where peace wraps around us,
each petal and each note,
cradling us till dawn calls us back,
to the faces we wear, to heat of the day.

But for now, we dream,
under this soft dark sky,
held gently by night, ready for rest,
for we will rise again,
To many roles of the day, with one tiny heart.

5. Eternal love of day and night

As the sun rises,
it paints orange and pink
across the canvas of the sky,
a gentle reminder
today is a fresh start,
a chance to dream again.

The day gently pushes darkness away,
chasing shadows into corners,
offering moments to craft,
to create, to choose,
to build a life,
step by step.

Every hour is a gift,
each minute a chance,
to fill our minds with light,
to gather laughter,
to soak in warmth,

before the sun beckons the
night so that it can rest.

When dusk rolls in,
if we've danced with purpose,
the stars sing a lullaby,
lulling our minds to peaceful dreams.
But waste the daylight in worry or doubt,
and the dark can become a fright,
reminding us of things undone,
those looming whispers of regret.

Day and night, a dance so sweet,
two partners, side by side,
each relying on the other,
as sunlight beckons starlight,
and the moon brushes the sky bright

It's a bond that breathes beauty,
teaching us with each cycle,
that treating the day with love,
will invite that same love,
to guide our nights,
and soothe our souls
for they are made for each other.

6. Coffee

Coffee, a sweet wonder on this earth,
whispers morning secrets as I lift the lid,
it's dark notes swirl into the air,
a love letter just for my senses,
turning dawn into something bright.

With careful hands, I cradle each scoop,
placing grounds in the filter,
the warm water bursts forth,
pours it's heart over those tiny gems,
slowly and so slowly

A dripping sound, like soft rain outside,
as my heart settles down
wrapped in rich aroma of rhythmic drips
waiting for my world to wake up.

In the pan, as the milk boils,
bubbles rise like hopeful arms,
a warm embrace waiting,

and when the dark coffee hits the light,
they swirl together, as if
they've been longing for one another.

Together they form a beautiful potion
creamy and magical, brings in the grace
to greet the day, to tackle tasks,
fuelling the rhythm of the day.

Time spent here with my coffee and him,
gentle laughter and shared sips,
time slows as each moment
sets the tune,
a melody of connection, so divine
setting the tone for the day so fine.

7. Music

Music is the magic
that lets us drift through time,
a gentle breeze stirring up
the echoes of laughter
and whispers of lovely moments.

Each note, takes
back to sunny days,
where joy danced in the air
and troubles were small like shadows.
It carries the warmth of memory,
the taste of nostalgia,
like an old photograph
that colors the grey.

In the quiet of the night,
music cradles the weary heart,
a soft hand on the shoulder,
whispering peace to the chaos.
It feeds the soul,

more than a feast for the ears.

On a long drive,
windows down, miles stretching,
music becomes the road itself,
shortening the distance between here
and the dreams waiting ahead.
It drapes our journey in melody,
filling the empty spaces
with every rhythm, every breath.

Oh, how it heals,
the tired weary soul,
lifting us from below
to float among the stars,
where worries fade,
lost in the notes of now.

8. Books - Gateway to wonderland

Books are the gateway to wonderland,
pages full of life and dreams,
their scent fills the air,
a mix of ink and adventure,
whispering secrets waiting to be found.

With each turn I step inside,
becoming hero and fool,
fighting villains with a flick of my finger,
or drifting through forests of magic
wonder waits on every line.

I'm a child again,
exploring worlds both strange and familiar,
dancing with dragons, taming storms,
my heart beats louder with each new tale.

Every story takes me far away,
to lands where anything is possible,

where courage blooms and friendships flourish,
where I'm not just a reader,
but a traveler in a world of endless possibilities.

Each day I dive into the pages,
growing with every word spoken,
a quiet strength appears within,
reminding me that life too,
is an adventure waiting only for
a courageous heart and bravery.

So give me the next book,
let me escape again in those words,
for books are the gateway to wonderland
a treasure trove of life I can hold,
living a thousand lives,
in the infinite pages that call me home.

9. School

In the halls of our second home,
where laughter echoes off worn walls,
we learn the art of friendship,
hands raised, voices bright,
building bonds that shape our lives.

Math and science line the blackboard,
but beneath the numbers and symbols,
we find the deeper lessons,
learning to share our stories,
to speak our hearts in tangled words.

Discipline rides on the morning bell,
and order brings comfort to our days,
as we discover the joy of playing fair,
of caring, of wearing smiles
like badges stitched with kindness.

Teachers, our guiding stars,
like mothers in wisdom's embrace,

carry our dreams within their hearts
they beam with pride,
echoing our achievements
throughout the life's quiet march.

This school teaches us to rise,
to meet the world with open hands,
to see the light that dispels the dark,
to challenge ignorance with knowledge,
and face life's brave adventures.

Here, we mould ourselves from clay,
underneath the fluorescent glare,
where every lesson is a stepping stone,
and every friend becomes a piece of home,
the foundation of who we'll become.

10. Sea

Oh Sea! so deep and vast,
I wonder what you hold,
What are the secrets and dreams,
If I could meet you,I'd ask,
"What do you seek,
as you touch the sky,
and reach toward the land".

Sun and moon find peace in you,
Their warm embrace reflects your joy,
Like a mother welcoming her children home, at each rise
and set,
A quiet dance of love returned,

Do you touch the clouds or do they come down,
Whispering soft tales only you can hear,
You stay so silent,
Guarding treasures we can only guess,
With wonders tucked beneath your waves.

I could sit and gaze at you all day,
Lose myself in your rhythm,
Forget the world as laughter fades,
The beauty of shells upon your shore,
Whispers of your grace by their
Hard outside and soft inside.

You hide pearls and mighty whales,
The moon's glow shines so bright,
Sharing secrets exchanged gently,
A tapestry of night woven in lullabies,
Your waves rise, then fall,
A heartbeat of life, a song of peace.

Oh, lovely sea, Your melody soothes my soul,
In every crest and trough, I find calm,
A gentle song that echoes,
Through all my restless thoughts,
You are the keeper of whispers,
Oh Sea! you are so deep and vast.

11. Perfectly Imperfect

Nature is perfectly imperfect,
each branch a twist, a turn,
no straight lines in this wild map,
yet leaves cluster has equal number
each stem wearing the same green dress.

One tree blooms with countless blossoms,
the same fruit brought forth,
each one cradled in rough hands of bark,
a reminder that beauty
comes in the soft chaos.

Birds fly like painted dreams,
no two alike, each feather a story,
a splash of color in a quiet sky,
each one celebrates its own song.

Rivers flow zigzag through stones,
never straight but always flowing forward,
each mountain stands proud,

with creases and curves,
their rugged faces telling tales of time.

We, too, are of different shapes,
five fingers stretch from each palm,
varied and unique,
yet only five on each hand.

Nature, the grand teacher of math and physics,
With a great art in its heart
perfect timing of the seasons,
the dance of day and night,
all painted in shades of rainbow colours.

Who are we to chase perfection
when we breathe in this gentle mess
Even I am perfectly imperfect ,
a piece of this wild, beautiful nature,
where flaws and wonders meet,
and everything has its own way to thrive.

12. Discipline and Dedication

With discipline in our hearts,
We navigate life's twists and parts.
Dedication fuels our fire,
Pushing us to aim higher.
Through challenges and strife,
They teach us the value of life.
Like a beacon in the night,
They lead us towards the light.
In moments of doubt and fear,
They whisper, "persevere."
To achieve our dreams,
Discipline and dedication are the means.
They require sacrifice and sweat,
But the rewards are surely met.
So let us embrace their call,
And rise above all.
For discipline and dedication,
Are the keys to transformation

13. Smile - The beautiful ornament

Smile, the gentle curve,
a simple twist that changes the mood,,
like sunlight breaking through a cloud,
warming hearts along the way.

It's the best ornament,
adorning faces with joy,
easy as a whisper,
it's free, a gift for all.

With this small act,
you turn frowns to laughter,
you heal wounds unseen,
bringing friends back together.

It has the magic power
to soften the heaviest day,
to calm storms brewing in minds,
and ease the burden of unspoken words

Each smile is a little medicine,
that makes life's meal sweeter,
helps us share just two more bites,
bringing us closer.

So smile, dear friend,
for this curve is a blessing,
a simple thread connecting us,
making everything right,
like a song shared through laughter.

14. Courage

Courage is not about the muscle flex
It's about the strength within, a fire that glows.
It's getting out of bed when you can't, you see,
When every fiber of your being wants to stay in bed, just
be.

It's waiting patiently even when the tide is against you,
When all hope seems lost and your dreams are fleeting
hue
It's having faith in self when the world around you says,
"You're not enough," and all your doubts and fears play.

Courage is that true self that spark within,
That tells you to keep going to rise above the din.
It's the voice that whispers "You got this," in your ear
The one that tells you to keep pushing, to have no fear.

So don't let anyone tell you that courage is just a
physical feat,
For it's much more than that, it's a state of being and a

soul treat.

Courage is the sum of all your hopes, your dreams, and your heart,

A strength that's innate, a power that sets you apart.

15. Faith

In realms unseen, where darkness reigns,
Faith shines like beacon, dispelling pains.
A guiding light that shines through,
lighting the path we're yet to pursue.

With faith as anchor, we brave the test,
And find solace in life's conflicting quest.
Through trials and errors we stride,
Unshaken by doubts, with heart full of pride.

It grants us courage, when fears sail,
to face challenges, and never fail.
Faith lifts our spirits, like wings so bright,
enabling us to shine like the morning light.

When uncertainty clouds our sight,
faith whispers assurance, get rid of endless night.
It stands by us, unwavering and true,
Empowering us to see this journey through.

Like an unbroken chain, it links us to our higher self,
binding heart and soul, right where we belong.
With every step, our trust takes hold,
and faith's sweet voice reminds us to be bold.

let us walk in faith, unshakeable and free,
embracing each dawn, wild and careless
For in its radiance, our path unfolds,
As faith bestows the strength, our hearts have been told.

16. Hope

Hope whispers secrets in twilight's embrace,
With gentle hands, it removes our fears,
Wiping away the remnants of tears,
Promising once more to find solace.

It sings in quiet tones beneath the stars,
The moon it's confidant in disguise
Each failure a lesson, not demise,
Guiding us past life's unyielding bars.

In shadows, hope becomes the morning sun,
A silent vow that echoes through the day,
Its warmth that dispels the cold,
Revealing paths of win assured.

Hope is that soft voice of the soul when night swoon
Don't worry, it says, we will rise again soon.
With faith as steady as the new moon,
We will try once more and reclaim our crown.

17. Change is a choice

Embrace the change that brings forth growth and light,
Let go of fear and step into the unknown, take flight.

Change for the better is a choice we make each day,
To leave behind the old, and pave a new way.

It may not be easy, it may be filled with strife,
But in the end, it leads to a better, brighter life.

So let us welcome change with open arms and heart,
For it is the only way to truly grow and start.

Embrace the unknown, embrace the new,
For change is the only way to see our dreams come true.

18. Freedom

I savored the release as chains fell from my mind,
Each thought a lock,
every duty a shackle unkind.

In this boundless expanse,
freedom I find,
To see flowers as flowers and thorns in their kind.

No longer forced to morph all I see or bind,
A free bird in this infinite sky,
unconfined.

Appreciating each essence,
with clarity defined,
For each has its place and purpose aligned.

The universe vast,
with sights intertwined,
I wander unhindered,
no longer maligned.

With truth in heart and peace consigned,
Embracing life's tapestry where beauty's enshrined.

Bound by none,
to my soul I've resigned,
Finding joy in simplicity as thoughts unwind.

Through clarity of vision,
understanding refined,
Every element treasured for the role designed

19. Solitude

Solitude is a silent companion we all must embrace
A journey into our own minds, a sacred space.

In solitude, we face our fears and doubts head on
We confront our weaknesses, until they are gone.

No distractions to pull us away from our thoughts
Only the sound of our heartbeat, our emotions wrought.

Solitude unveils our deepest desires and dreams
It shows us the way, or so it seems.

Alone, but not lonely, in the quiet of our soul
We find peace and clarity, our minds made whole.

In solitude, we learn to appreciate our own company
To cherish the moments of quiet, of tranquility.

We unravel the mysteries of our own existence
And find solace in our own resistance.

Solitude teaches us to be comfortable in our skin
To embrace the solitude, and let our true selves in.
34

So let us not fear the quiet, the stillness of our mind
For in solitude, our true selves we will find.

20. Dream

A dream whispers secrets in the night,
A dance upon the moon's silver wings,
It sings of futures to be unfold,
Guiding heart with gentle might.

It paints the sky with colors unseen,
Stars bow to it's mighty will,
In slumber's embrace, it softly calls,
To meets where only thoughts gather.

With every breath it weaves a nest,
Hope and fear that together spring,
From dusk till dawn it ever flows,
Restlessness fuelled by twilight.

It stands as guard against despair's veil
Giving courage to climb that hill,
To chase the horizons undefined,
Dreams teach us to stand up tall.

21. Life and Death

he Breath of Now

In the cradle of dawn, where life takes its flight,
We breathe in the whispers of hope's gentle light,
Each heartbeat a rhythm, a dance on the cusp,
Of a fragile existence, of dreams wrapped in trust.

We gather the moments like petals from flowers,
Both sorrow and joy, in their sweetest of hours,
But few will engrave in the echoes of time,
The love that we foster, the hearts that we bind.

So live with intention, embrace every spark,
The laughter, the tears, the light in the dark,
For passion ignites us, a fire within,
A purpose, a journey that starts with that breath.

With every "I love you" that dances on lips,
In kindness extended, let gratitude slip,
For too soon, the curtain is drawn with a sigh,

And the echoes of silence will cradle the sky.

Don't wait for the dusk to adorn them with praise,
Let them feel your warmth in the soft light of days,
For when lives fade to shadows, it's us who will tire,
From the flames of regrets that extinguish our fire.

So celebrate loudly, as each moment unfolds,
Embrace the real beauty, their stories retold,
For the lives that we cherish, and those that we grieve,
Are stitched in the fabric of how we believe.

Love them now, in their essence, their flaws and their
grace,
For in every encounter, we dance, we embrace,
And when the breath whispers softly its last,
We'll carry their light as we step from the past.

Life's a fleeting shadow, a canvas of grace,
We etch our intentions, our stories, our face,
Yet death is a mirror reflecting our days,
Two sides of a coin in this infinite maze.

22. New Poem

www.ingramcontent.com/pod-product-compliance
Lightning Source LLC
Chambersburg PA
CBHW070611160726
48003CB00005B/2214